Remembering Our Baby

A workbook for children whose brother or sister died

By Patti Keough

Design by Janet Sieff, Centering Corporation

ISBN: 1-56123-140-1
San: 298-1815

Centering Corporation
PO BOX 4600 Omaha, NE 68104
Phone: 866-218-0101 Fax: 402-553-0507

Email: j1200@aol.com
Online catalog: www.centering.org

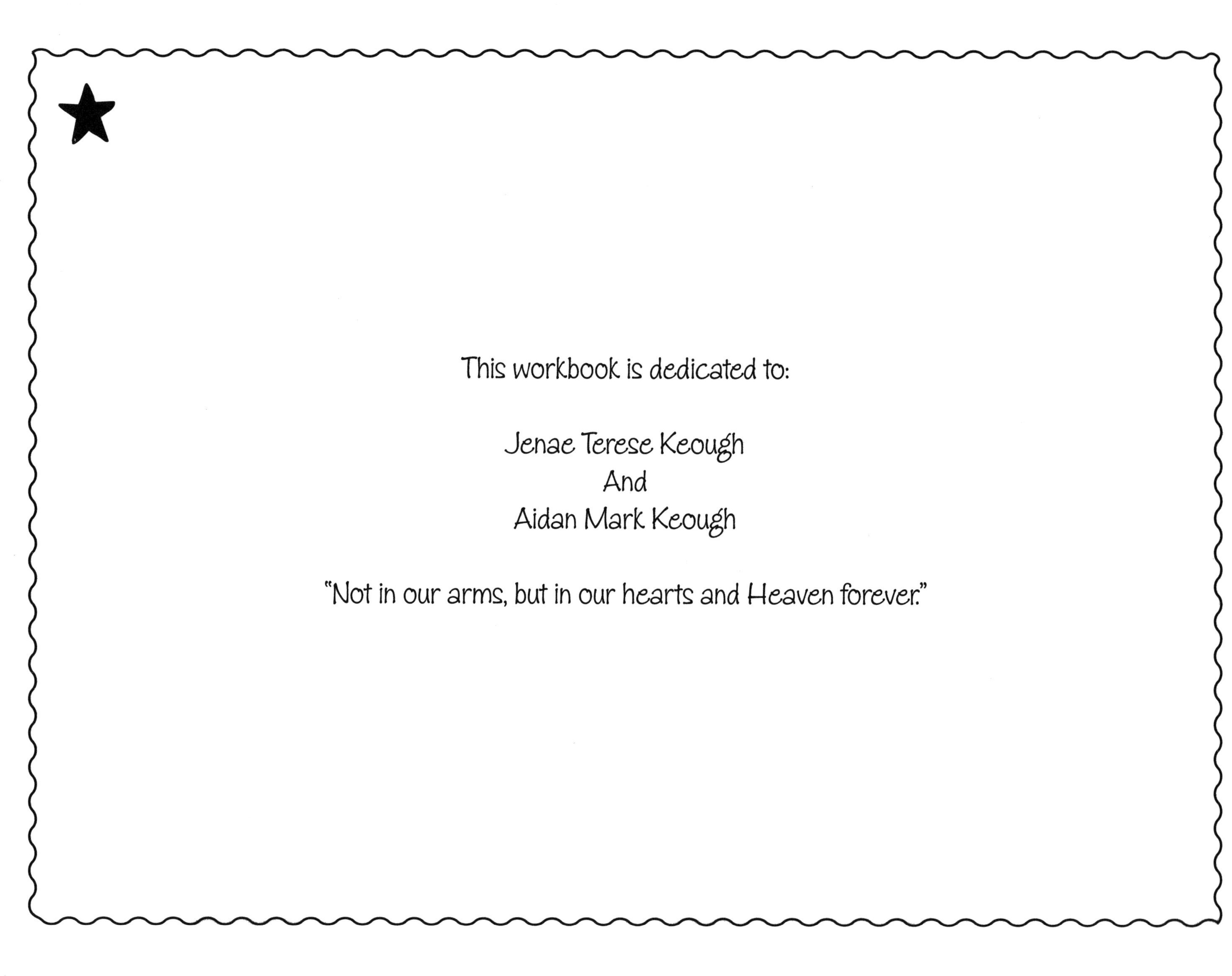

This workbook is dedicated to:

Jenae Terese Keough
And
Aidan Mark Keough

"Not in our arms, but in our hearts and Heaven forever."

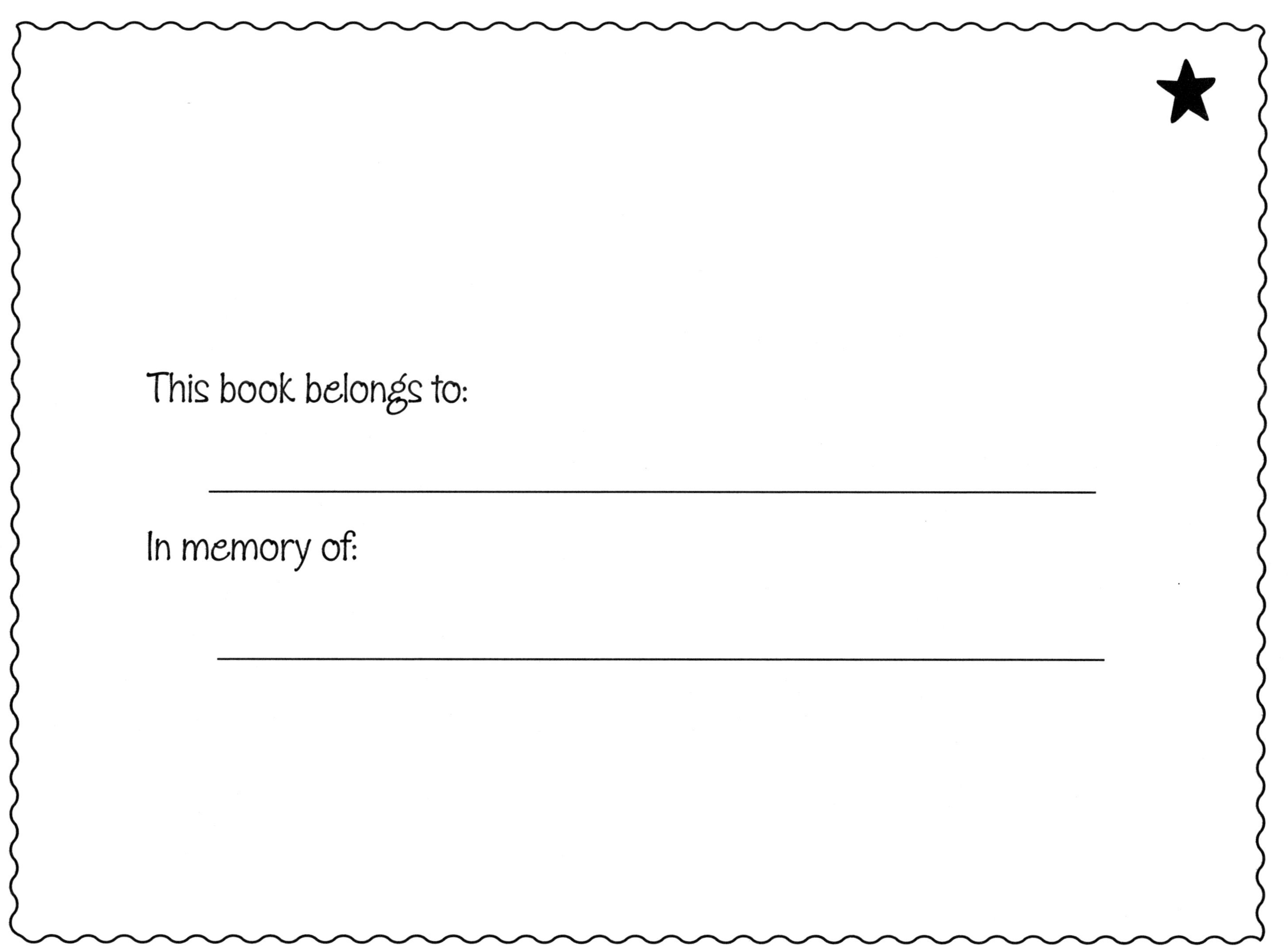

This book belongs to:

____

In memory of:

____

This is your book

This book is for you if your baby sister or brother died before birth.
You may write and draw on the pages.

Writing and drawing will help you share your thoughts and feelings.

While you are working in this book (or when you are all done) show it to someone who is special to you.

You can talk about it together.

When my Mommy and Daddy first told me we were going to have another baby in our family I felt . . .

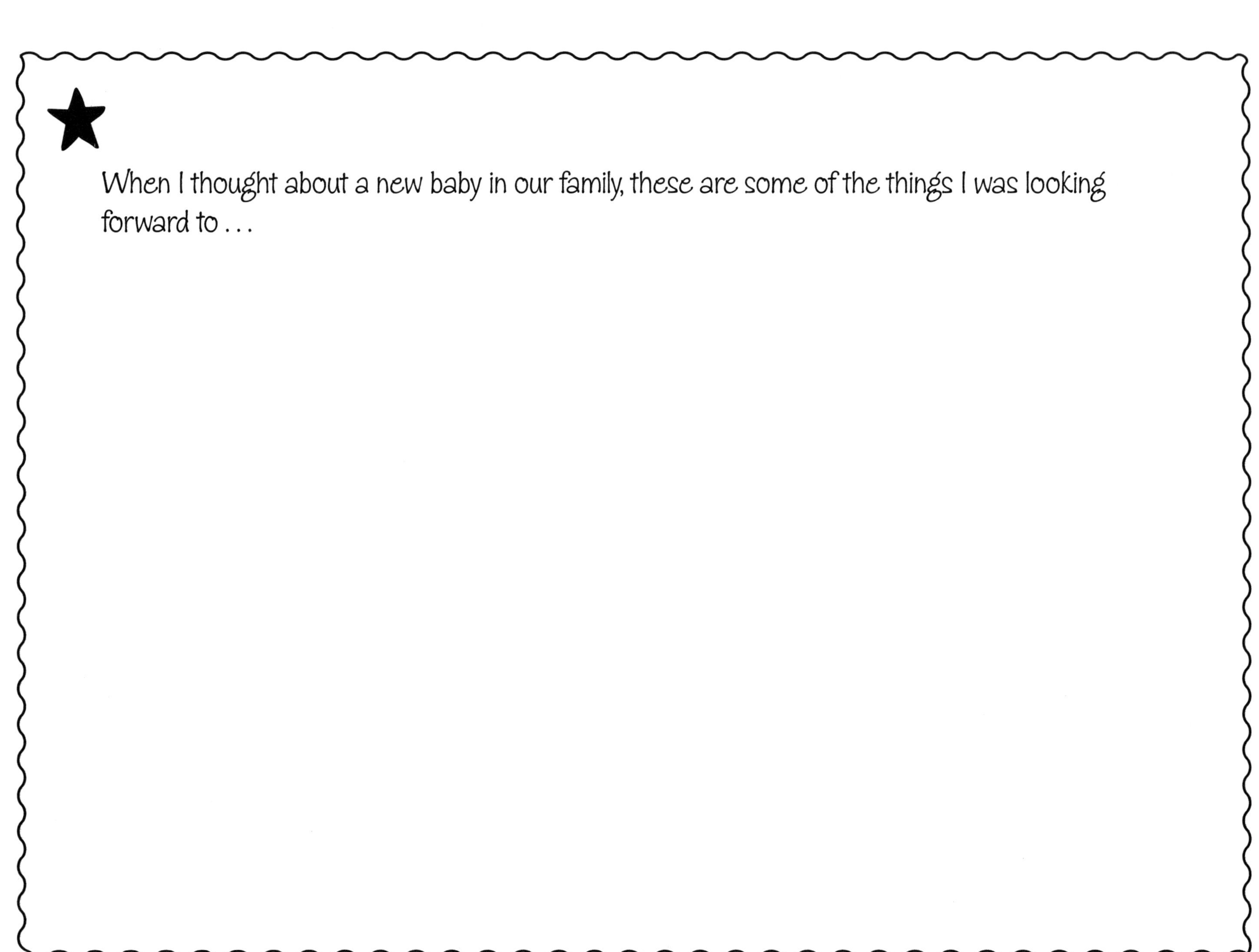

When I thought about a new baby in our family, these are some of the things I was looking forward to . . .

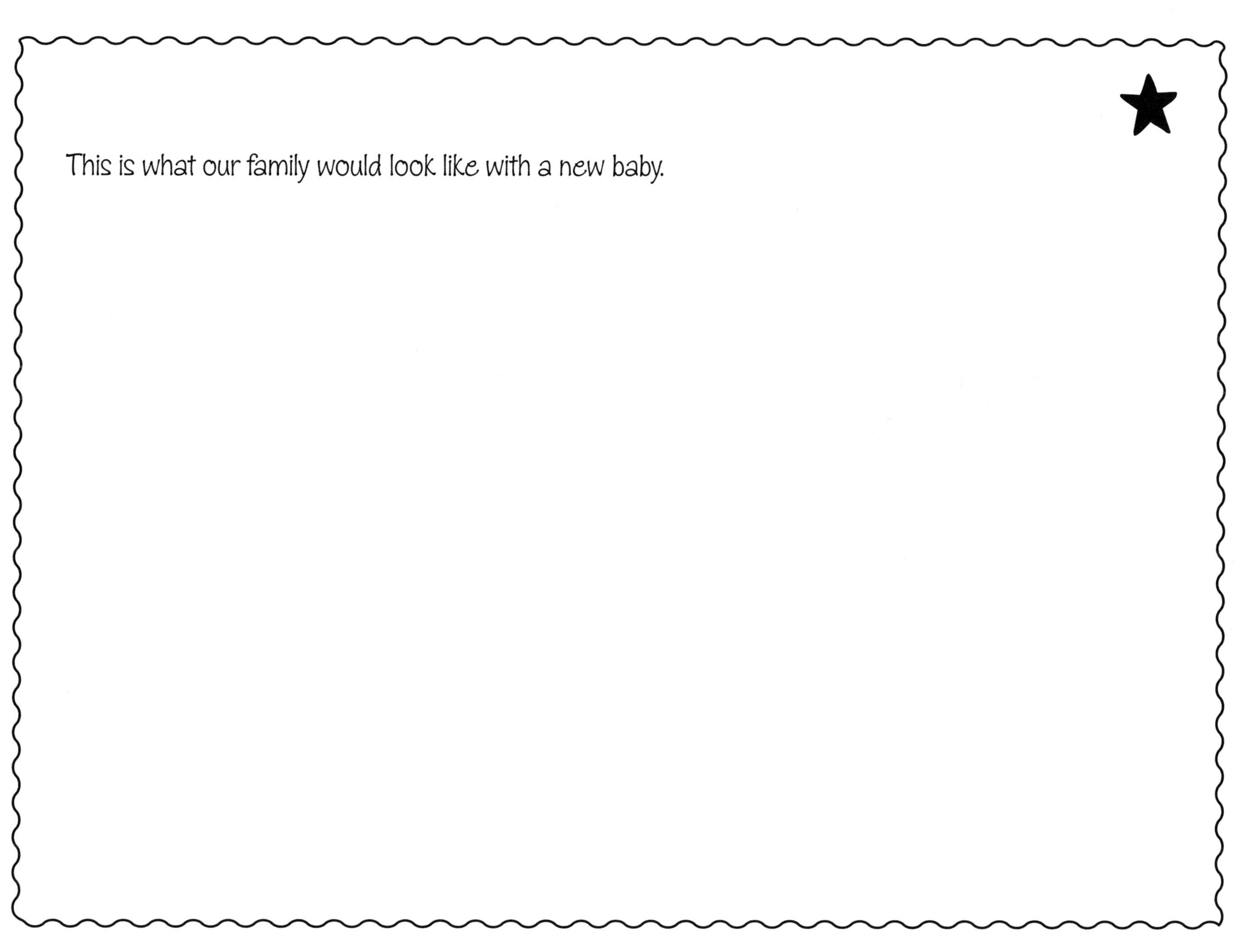
This is what our family would look like with a new baby.

Then one day my Mommy and Daddy told me our baby had died. It was hard for me to understand. Mommy told me not everything or everyone lives a full life.

If you plant seeds in the dirt, many of them grow, but some die in the ground.

Of all the colorful buds on a rose bush, most of them blossom into beautiful flowers, but some never open up. They die closed tight.

Even most caterpillars turn into pretty butterflies, but some are not strong enough to break out of their cocoon.

After I heard our baby died I felt . . .

Mommy and Daddy said even though our baby died before birth, we could still give the baby a name. We decided to name our baby ______________________________

Because . . .

I think if our baby was born alive, our baby would look like this . . .

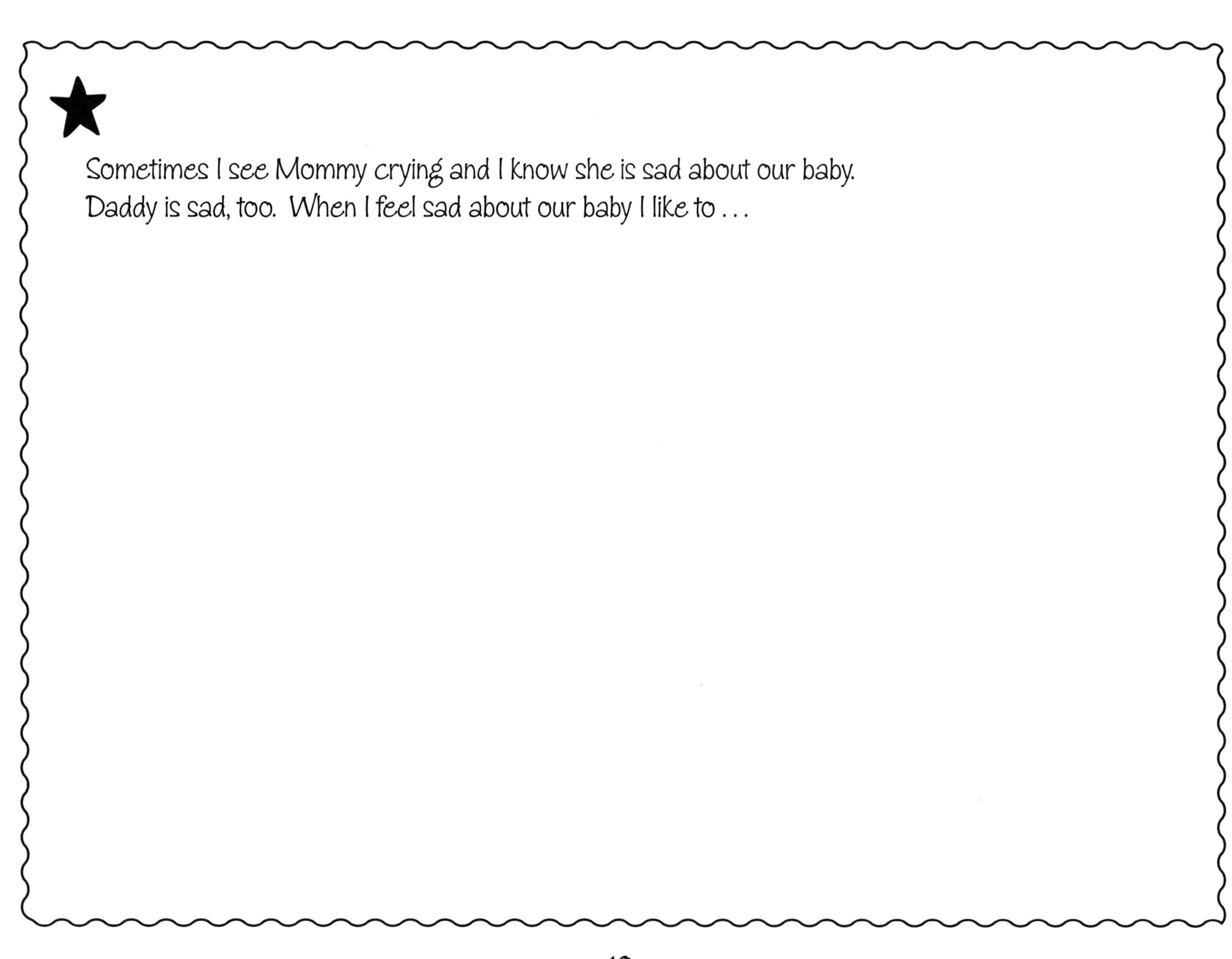

Sometimes I see Mommy crying and I know she is sad about our baby. Daddy is sad, too. When I feel sad about our baby I like to . . .

Even though we're sad, we're still a family no matter what. This is what I love about my family . . .

If I could talk to our baby today I would say . . .

Other people have had babies who die. Sometimes they choose a special way to remember their baby like…

Planting a tree for the baby

Having a memorial service

Getting a special teddy bear to hold

Wearing a piece of jewelry that reminds them of the baby

Getting a Christmas ornament to hang on the tree

Lighting a Yahrzeit (memorial) candle on the anniversary of the death

Putting a new picture on the wall

Keeping a silk flower arrangement out on a table

Having an "our baby" candle to burn at any time

Doing something special on the baby's due date

There are lots of ways to remember a baby.

I would like to remember our baby by . . .

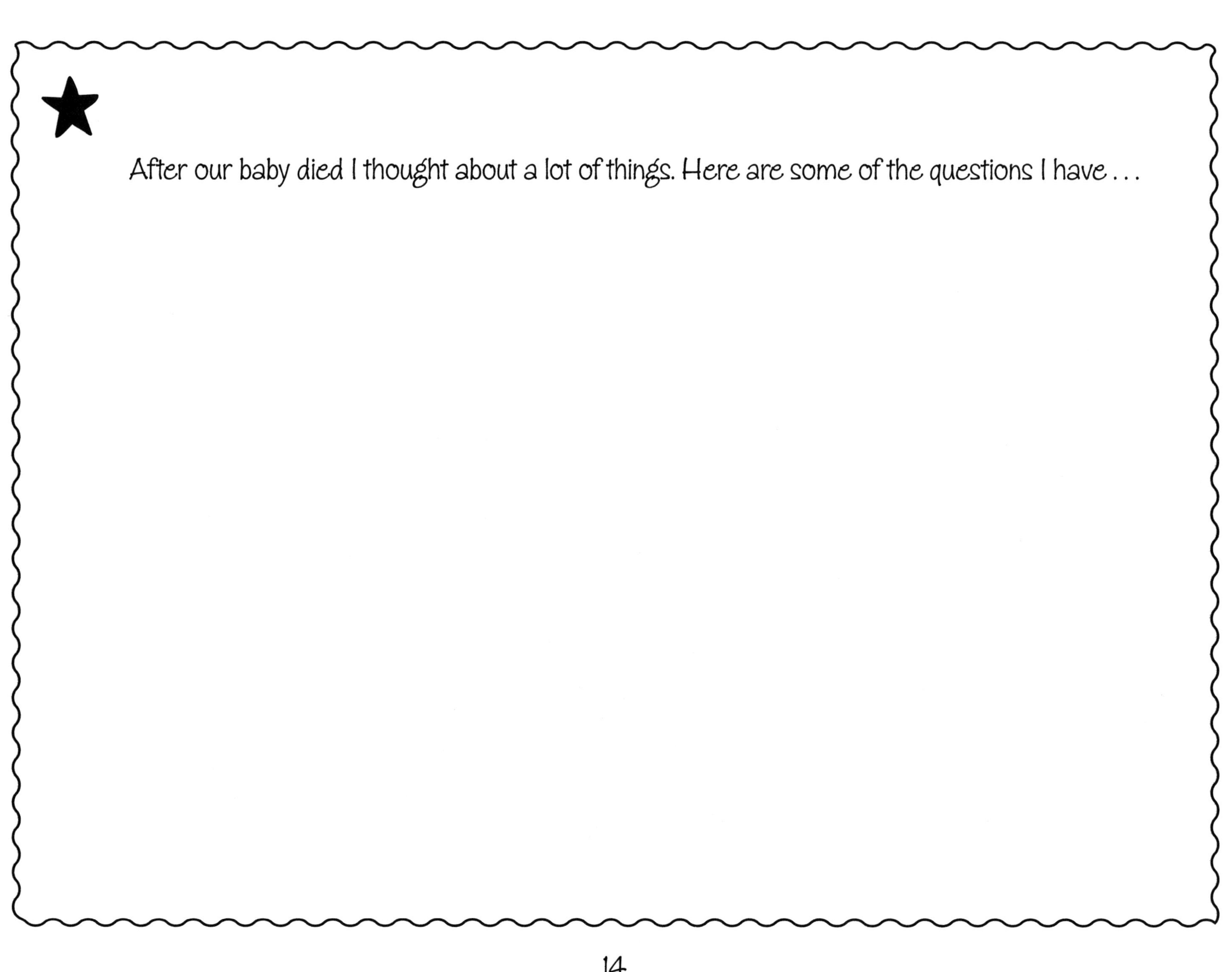

After our baby died I thought about a lot of things. Here are some of the questions I have . . .

Even though our baby died, there are still many people and things in my life I am thankful for. Some of these people and things are . . .

About the Author

Patti Keough lives in Arizona with her husband Mark and three children-Terese, Kathryn and Justin.

After her second miscarriage, Patti designed this workbook to help her children With their grief. A certified Grief Facilitator, Patti has worked in the field of bereavement for 14 years. She founded The Christy Center for Loss and Renewal in Mesa, AZ, which provides grief support groups for children, teens and adults.